T0209579

W.A.R.
(WOMEN IN ABUSIVE RELATIONSHIPS)

A SPIRITUAL JOURNEY

Dr. V. W. Taylor PhD

WESTBOW
PRESS®
A DIVISION OF THOMAS NELSON
& ZONDERVAN

WestBow Press books may be ordered through booksellers or by contacting:

WestBow Press
A Division of Thomas Nelson & Zondervan
1663 Liberty Drive
Bloomington, IN 47403
www.westbowpress.com
844-714-3454

All Scripture quotations are taken from the King James Version.

ISBN: 978-1-6642-6544-8 (sc)
ISBN: 978-1-6642-6543-1 (e)

Library of Congress Control Number: 2022908101

Print information available on the last page.

WestBow Press rev. date: 05/02/2022

Contents

Introduction

Women in **A**busive **R**elationships (WAR). This is the perfect name because women in abusive relationships are essentially in a *war* with the enemy every day. Just like any war, there are good days and bad days, but it is a constant fight for survival. This is a battle women go through every morning when they wake up until the time they lay their heads down to sleep at night. Each WAR is different, whether it is neglectful (the spouse is not home much and leaves the woman open and vulnerable), physical (the spouse puts his hands on the woman, throws objects at or in the direction of the woman), emotional (the spouse constantly puts down the woman, spouse is very controlling), or a combination. All of them end up being spiritual battles. It is a spiritual journey down a long, broken, and beaten road.

It is one thing to be unequally yoked in a marriage to a decent man, but it is an entirely different story if the man is an abuser. There may be some men who try to use religion against you or throw it in your face. "Wives, submit yourselves to your own husbands as you do to the Lord. For the husband is the head of the church, his body, of which he is the Savior. Now as the church submits to their husbands in everything" (Ephesians 5:22–24 NIV). Some men take this scripture out of context. This does not mean that the husband is the authoritarian in the relationship, and you must obey his orders. The Lord made Eve for Adam as a companion for the man so he would not be alone in his daily life; she was not made to be his slave. For women of God, this really puts us in an awkward position because we are being pulled in two different directions.

The first rule of thumb is that if you recognize signs of abuse prior to getting married, most likely it will not change once you get married. It may possibly get worse because he will think he owns you. Sometimes, the abusive behaviors may not be apparent until after the marriage. This is where women begin to feel pulled in different directions. Your heart is with your husband, and you want to be a good, godly, submissive wife, but your morals and beliefs pull you in the opposite direction, when you feel like your husband should be showing you love and respect also. "Husbands, love your wives, even as Christ loved the church and gave himself up for her" (Ephesians 5:25). When a husband and wife come together, they are to become as one. This means working together to help and support each other in every way possible: physically, mentally, emotionally, and spiritually. I don't think some people actually absorb and take in the vows they say to one another in marriage: "to love and to cherish." Nowhere in the vows does it say anything about the man treating the woman badly and disrespectfully. Women's ways of expressing love and an abusive man's way of expressing love are two totally opposite ways. If the two ways are not working together, something is wrong. What will you choose?

The second rule of thumb is that you will have to make

a choice: either continue to live with the abuse or make a change. The change will first have to happen within yourself prior to anything else happening. Once you have made that change inside, then you will be able to handle and decide about the changes that will happen around you. That final decision will be between you and the Lord. You will also need to decide what you will do with your life after your transformation takes place inside.

Keep this in mind: every relationship is different, and every outcome will be different. Some relationships may last while others don't, but either way if you allow the transformation to take place in you, the Lord will guide you in the right direction. I hope that this book puts you on the right path to a more intimate relationship with God because He is your true guide to having inner peace in whatever you decide.

So often we spend time trying to either overcome or hide our weaknesses. But in our weaknesses are the very places God wants to display His power in our lives. In scriptures, we are encouraged to embrace our weaknesses and through them experience a power that we could never know otherwise. In 2 Chronicles 20, we acknowledge weakness in order to experience God's strength. It is when we are in our weakness that we find ourselves and find the strength in the Lord. In Jeremiah 18:3, the Lord is the potter, and we are the clay. The Lord will spin the wheel as slowly or as quickly as He wants. The Lord is in control of the circumstances and, depending on how the Lord plans on using us, determines the circumstances we will encounter.

In the Book of Daniel, Meshach, Shadrach, and

Abednego were thrown into the fiery furnace for not following the king's orders and bowing down to the statue. But in the story, the Lord did not keep them out of the furnace; instead, the Lord led them through it without harm. This is what the Lord will do for us. He will allow trials in our lives, but He will walk us through them. This poem, called "Fake Smile," that I wrote basically describes how women in abusive relationships may feel inside while trying to hide those feelings on the outside.

I put a fake smile on my face
Hoping what I feel inside doesn't replace
I try to make it through the day
This burden I carry is weighing me down
Hope my smile doesn't turn to a frown
Please help me, Lord, make it through the day
So, I can safely say
What is coming next
I will never know
Because when I walk through the door
Which way will I be directed to go
But I continue to pray
So, I can safely say
Thank you, Lord
For carrying me through another day.

Chapter One

The Low Point in Life and the Beginning of the Spiritual Journey

||||||||||||||||||||||||

I grew up knowing the Lord, but for some unfounded reason, I always chose the wrong men to be in relationships with, or they were just not ready for the commitment I wanted. During all this time, I thought I was growing in Christ, until temptation got the best of me. I was alone, raising five children, and I got lonely. I should have used this time to draw closer to God, and I thought I was, but obviously my mind was set on other things.

I knew what I wanted in a man, but I was only looking at the outside cover not the inside, which is the most important piece. I would call myself a surface Christian: my faith was displayed on the outside. I wanted a man who would go to church with me, and who would accept my children and be a protector, as I was having problems with my ex. The man I thought would fulfill these requirements was a retired police officer. Little did I know that would come back to haunt me. All of that hope was short lived after I said, "I do." In the beginning, we all went to church together, and went on bike rides and hikes in the mountains. It was fun and enjoyable, even for the children at first, but things slowly got worse. Remember one thing: surface faith will not be sufficient when circumstances threaten what you treasure most in life (Dooley 2020); for me, that was and is my children.

This is probably how it happens most of the time. The men don't want to show their true colors before they have you, because then you can always back out; after "I do," it is more difficult to leave, especially when children are involved. Honestly, I probably saw some signs of his true colors before getting married, but I did not want to think the worst, and inside I was probably scared of being alone again. Second Timothy 3:2–6 talks about how in the last days, people will be abusive and without self-control. It states that they will wiggle their way into homes and gain control over gullible women. This has been taking place, and will continue until the end of time. I know we never want to think of ourselves as gullible, but when the Lord is not first in our hearts, it leaves room for the serpent to creep his way in. The devil knows our weaknesses. Do not ever think you can hide them from God or the devil.

I honestly thought I was a strong woman to be raising five kids on my own and keeping it all together. I had recently lost my mother, who was my best friend, prior to having my fifth child. I had bought a house for my children and myself. I did not realize how weak I was until I allowed a wolf in sheep's clothing to take over my life. This trial helped to open my eyes, and reveal my weakness and how much I truly needed the Lord. When things are going well, we do not feel that the Lord is needed, at least not to the point that we are dependent upon Him to make it through the day. I became so dependent on the Lord for the strength to make it through each day. Second Peter 1:5 says we must strengthen our lives so we will be unshakeable and firm in the midst of suffering.

Not long after getting married, I lost my job and was truly at the lowest point in my life. This is where the spiritual journey began. Isaiah 41:10 tells us not to fear even in our brokenness; God will give us strength and hold us up when we can't hold ourselves up. Looking back, if you already think you're a strong person in Christ, how can God move in your life without first breaking you down? My foundation was weak, so it was only a matter of time before the house crumbled. It's in our weakest moments that God shows His strength. That is why, for Christ's sake, I delight in weaknesses, in insults, in hardships, in persecutions, and in difficulties. "For when I am weak, then I am strong" (2 Corinthians 12:10).

The Lord must allow us to reach a low point in our lives sometimes; when we are at our weakest and most vulnerable, we are able to have a deeper relationship with Him. Humans tend to be naturally stubborn, so if someone says anything to us while things are going well, it probably goes in one ear and out the other. It isn't until we are at a loss and at our lowest that we finally listen. This is when we are open to receiving the Lord's help and guidance, and at this point, we finally let go and let God take over. When we are at our weakest, the Spirit can transform us into Christ's image. For me, it was when I lost my job and felt like I was going to lose everything. I felt like I had lost control of my life. I had children to take care of and a mortgage to pay; how in the world was I going to do that? I'd just gotten married too, and I was sure he was thinking, *Great. Now I have to take care of everyone! Oh no!*

I have always been a structured person, but after losing my job, I became unglued. This trial has disciplined me to become more devoted to the Lord. I know that every abusive relationship varies in some way, but no matter what, the abuser's goal is to keep women feeling helpless, worthless, and weak. The enemy is trying to defeat us. "The thief comes only to steal and kill and destroy" (John 10:10 NIV). God has won for us and has given us the authority to overcome all powers of the enemy (Luke 10:19). "But the Lord is faithful, he will strengthen you and guard you from the evil one" (2 Thessalonians 3:3 NLT). "And the peace of God, which transcends all understanding, will guard your hearts and your minds in Christ Jesus" (Philippians 4:7 NIV).

During this low point in my life, I worked different jobs, trying to keep my head above water and not lose my house. After nine months of being married, I became pregnant with our daughter. Even during my pregnancy, things were violent, and he would threaten to leave me. Of course, being the "godly" woman, I was determined to keep this marriage together. I had already been divorced two times; I did not want strike three against me. I thought, *I can make him a better man. I know the Lord can change him.* In the beginning of our relationship, the abuse was definitely more physical; then it gradually turned toward emotional abuse. People don't realize how hurtful words can be. James 3:6 states that the tongue is evil and corrupts the body. What people, especially your husband or significant other, say can be very hurtful to hear when it is nothing nice to the ears. Sometimes we are not able to walk away or free ourselves from toxic people (at least not at a particular time), but this is when we must become stronger than we ever have been (Thomas 2019).

We continued to attend church together because that was my thing during my pregnancy— "we have to go to church together." Then our daughter was born, and for a few months, I did not go to church at all. I felt like something was missing in my life by not going to church, and I thought, *Why am I going to let someone keep me from going to church?* My husband didn't want to go, and I wanted to keep the peace, so I stayed home also.

When our daughter was three months old, I found a promising job as a teaching assistant. I had a Bachelor of Science degree in Health and Physical Education with a concentration in athletic training. I had taught in a public school setting for three years, but I was totally turned off toward teaching, so I stopped and became a case manager for over ten years. Then the Lord opened the door for me to get back into the teaching field. I started as a teaching assistant because my teaching certificate had expired. Not long after getting the job as a teaching assistant, I decided to pursue and actually finish my master's degree. I had attempted two other times but ended up stopping due to issues with my home life. This time, I decided to do it online. I went back to school and got my Master's in Psychology, since this was the field that had always interested me. While I was taking classes for my master's, I attended the local community college online to complete the reading courses needed to renew my teaching certificate. For my sake and my children's, I needed to get back on my feet so I could afford everything on my own if needed. I was determined to finish this time. It was only through God's grace and strength that I was able to complete school despite everything that was going on in my home life.

There are times when we will have to make some hard decisions, but they are needed. Honestly, if we are making decisions that are favored by the Lord's will, we will be able to accomplish them. This decision to finish my master's degree was needed because I knew I had to get extra money to be able to take care of my children and myself. I did not care if my husband did not approve. I did have to do most of my schoolwork at my job, so I would get to work early to work on my schoolwork, and then I would work on it when he was not at home. When you're in this type of situation with a person who is controlling, you quickly learn what you can do and when you can do it depending on the mood and environment in the home.

This was a mild point in our relationship because he worked for the union downtown. They worked some weird hours. They worked early in the morning to set up the stages for the concerts, plays, and other events, and then late at night to take it all down, which worked out great for me. He left before me in the morning and would be getting ready to leave when I got home. Then he would get home in the early morning just before I had to get up for work. It didn't leave much time to argue, and he would be tired, so it was peaceful for a while.

I completed the reading courses in two semesters and was able to get my teaching certificate back, which was great. After my certification went through, I was called into the director's office at work, and I was offered the health and physical education teacher position because the current teacher was leaving. That wasn't just perfect, that was God's timing. Just a few months after starting my teaching position, I completed my Master's in Psychology. I was so excited and proud of myself. This was another steppingstone completed.

My husband would go through these cycles where he would be nice and kind, then he would go on his rampages. I'm sure like other abusive relationships, I felt like I was constantly walking on eggshells at home, never knowing what to expect while trying not to trigger a rampage. After completing my master's, he did encourage me to get my doctorate. I began looking into colleges to see which one had a suitable major and doctorate program.

Two months after completing my master's, I began my Doctorate in the Study of Advanced Human Behaviors. This turned out to be a long process, but well worth it now that I have completed it. During this stage, I continued to grow in the Lord even though things at home continued to get worse.

Adam B. Dooley states that sometimes our trials are related to, or are the consequences of, our sinful choices, but other times they may not have anything to do with our actions. Either way, they are intended to produce greater holiness. There is a purpose and plan behind every trial we suffer. Our objective is to get out of them what the Lord intends to teach us. I know for some of us this is a hard concept to grasp, and it may take a few rounds before we get it, but hopefully not. I was one of them. The final round was the most difficult, but it finally got my attention and opened my eyes. As Dooley states, "trials force us to move beyond superficial knowledge of Jesus into a meaningful, daily walk with Him" (Dooley 2020, 2). This couldn't be truer.

My husband quit his job with the union, so this meant he was home all the time. It meant he had more time to think about things, which was not good. From the start, my husband always had trouble sleeping. At night was when his brain went wild. Anything that happened during the day that he did not like, it all came out at night. I, on the other hand, am an early to bed and early to rise person. I would be in bed asleep, and he would come in the bedroom and start yelling at me about something my kids did, or something I said in the past. He had a problem with letting things go—he couldn't do it. He would be intentionally loud in order to wake up all the kids. He was very spiteful.

As I continue to say throughout, all abusive relationships vary, but most of them seem to go through cycles. For me, my husband would go on a rampage and then he would buy me clothes or something for the house either later that day or the next day. I guess it was his way of apologizing without having to say he was sorry. His abusiveness didn't just stop once I left the house for work every day; it would continue as I was driving to and from work and sometimes while I was at work. He would call me and begin yelling at me, cussing at me, calling me names, threatening to destroy some of my property or my kids' stuff before I got home. Most of the time, it was over past events or events in my past that happened before we even met. He would constantly throw my past marriages or things that I did in the past in my face all the time. He would try to belittle me because I had children from a different marriage. He constantly tried to make me feel like I was a low life, a worthless person, and a horrible mother.

At first when he would yell at me, I would yell back; when he became violent, I would be violent, because I wasn't going to let him think he could do this without me fighting back. He would threaten to destroy things he knew I enjoyed or that meant something to me. If he was mad enough, he would throw things—food, water, or objects—at me while I was in bed. I would throw things back at him, or throw his things on the floor. It got quite messy. He could not stand if I did the same thing to him; honestly, it probably made him angrier, but I didn't care. I was not going to let him think he could just walk all over me without repercussions. Things would eventually calm down around two or three in the morning because he would finally fall asleep, but I had to get up at 4:00 a.m. to get ready for work.

As I think back, I ask myself *why*. Why was I allowing him to change the person I am? I am not a spiteful person. I am not a violent person, but that was exactly how I was behaving. His toxicity and evilness were beginning to creep into me. I did not like it!

According to Gary Thomas, we do not want to get to the point where the other person's toxic nature seeps into us, but that was exactly what was happening when I became destructive like him. I did not like that feeling, so I stopped responding at his lower level. We cannot control what other people say and do, but we can control our behavior and how we respond to a given situation (Thomas, 2019). James 1:2–4 discusses how encountering trials produces patience. God allows us to go through trials to help strengthen our faith and build character (Dooley, 2020).

I know each relationship is different. Whether you are in a relationship with a person who does not care how he or she talks to you in public, or puts on a show to make it look like you are a happy couple, neither one is good. Either you are going to be embarrassed to be around the person in public, or you are left lying about how your relationship truly is. Both put you in a bad situation. In Romans 12:9, we read "let love be without dissimulation. Abhor that which is evil; cleave to that which is good." My husband would be affectionate and hold my hand to make it look like we were happy because he did not want people to know how he was behind closed doors. He was phony and fake, especially in front of other people. If we were out and he did not want to display any affection, he would stay away from me while we were out. That is what happened when we went on vacation one year.

This vacation was to Outer Banks, and it turned out to be a not so pleasant vacation. Throughout the entire vacation, I took the kids my way and he went his own way. One night, he went on a rampage, complaining about everything and anything. Then he began dumping all my hygiene products that I brought for the trip into the sink and trash. I was tired of him always ruining everything and being so spiteful, so I jumped on him from behind. He elbowed me right in my mouth and split my lip. Of course, he said it was my fault that this even occurred. I had to find an urgent care clinic and ended up getting seventeen stitches in my mouth total, some on the inside of my mouth and some on the outside. What fun, right? Of course, the nurses questioned me about what happened, and I lied and said that it was an accident. They failed to realize that first, we did not live there but were on vacation, and second, we drove there together. The last thing I needed was to have the cops investigating and make it worse on me later.

At times, why do we feel like we must fight back? Is it to prove a point? Is it really worth it? Does it really solve anything? Where does it leave us in the end? "A soft answer turneth away wrath: but grievous words stir up anger. The tongue of the wise useth knowledge aright: but the mouth of fools poureth out foolishness" (Proverbs 15:1–2). Sometimes it takes more guts and faith not to fight back (Furtick, 2019).

On the last day of our vacation, I took the kids to the beach. I set up the towels by a man sitting in a chair. I did not want to be around anybody because of the stitches in my mouth. I did not want people looking at me. The kids were playing by the water, but I had our daughter with me on the beach. I was worn out from the week of playing different roles, trying to keep the peace in the house, but also trying to let the kids have an enjoyable vacation—all while I was miserable. I ended up dozing off (I know I sound like a terrible parent) and when I woke up, our daughter was not in front of me. I looked around and saw this guy (the one who was in the chair I spoke of earlier) holding her hand and walking back to me. I ran over and got her, and thanked the man for bringing her back. My heart was pounding. I was overwhelmed with emotions because I felt like a horrible parent for not watching my child, but at the same time I also had a sense of peace because I knew she was fine. When I got back to our towels, I turned around to thank the guy again, but he had vanished. I did not even see him walking away. He disappeared. I thanked the Lord; even in the midst of the chaos and ugliness, the Lord sent His angel to watch over me and give me strength when I was at the end of mine. The man did not say one word; he did not criticize or judge me for my bad parenting. He completely vanished. He was my angel at that moment and my daughter's. The Bible does not teach that God helps those who help themselves; it teaches that God will help those who are truly at the end of themselves, whether they lack strength, or they feel unsafe, or they are totally lost (Mohler, 2018). "Hear my prayer, O, Lord and let my cry come unto thee. Hide not thy face from me in the day when I am in trouble; incline thine ear unto me: in the day when I call answer me speedily" (Psalm 102:1–2). That is exactly what happened. My soul was crying out to the Lord, and He helped me quickly.

This is when things started to change for me. The Lord began to open my eyes and show me that I did not have to drop down to his level to prove a point. Also, I did not want him to change the person I am inside. He had already secluded me enough from my family; I was not going to allow him to take away me. I have always been a structured person, but this trial disciplined and made me more committed to the Lord. Experiencing this trial caused me to be more devoted to reading scripture and studying His Word. I decided to take a nosedive into surrounding myself with godly people, listening to godly words every day, and reading the Word and devotionals daily.

God's Love
God's love is all around
It doesn't have to be found
It's the beautiful flowers that bloom
It's the stars and the moon
It's the bright sun in the sky
It's the birds as they fly
All we have to do is open up our eyes
We take this all for granted
Because we did not make this planet
How much love does God have to show?
Before we realize which way to go
I hope you don't wait until it's too late
So you can walk through those pearly gates

Thank You Lord

Chapter Two

Surround Yourself with Godly People and His Word

||||||||||||||||||||||

Every morning, I would get up to exercise a little, then change and get ready to leave for work. At times, I would rather be at work than home. It was my escape. The work environment was more relaxed than my home environment. In some abusive relationships, the man does not want the woman to work so he can be in complete control of every aspect of the woman's life. But a person can still surround himself or herself with the Lord in many ways.

During this stressful time in my life, I began to feel like I wanted and needed more. I decided to take a new lease on life. I was going to change my routine. Even through my suffering, I wanted to serve God's people more (Dooley, 2020). I have always believed in prayer, so I asked my supervisor if I could start a prayer group at work in the morning before the school day started. My supervisor was all for it. He said we could always use a lift before we started the day. I invited some coworkers who I knew would be interested in joining us. We would pray for individuals, situations, concerns, and work. It seemed to touch lives, and people began to put in prayer requests. This turned out to be such an uplifting start to the day. I loved it.

This was a great start in surrounding myself with the Lord. I got a taste of the Lord before I left my house in the morning by reading the Word and devotionals. I eventually started sending out a devotion to some friends and family each morning when I felt like it would touch some people. They would ask where it was if I did not send one that day, so this became my new thing. I began sending a devotion to family and friends each morning. My list of recipients continues to grow, which is such a blessing. When I hear of people being touched by the readings that I send, it is just another encouraging factor to help me get through what I am currently going through. Then I got to start my morning at work with prayer.

Then the Lord placed a woman in my life who helped me through a lot. Ms. Arwilda is a godly woman, who understood what I was going through because she went through a similar relationship. She would always give me encouraging words and scriptures. "He comforts us in all our troubles so that we can comfort others. When they are troubled, we will be able to comfort and give them the same comfort God has given us" (2 Corinthians 1:4 NLT). I remember the day she gave me the scripture in Jeremiah 29:11 (NIV): "For I know the plans I have for you, declares the Lord, plans to prosper you and not to harm you, plans to give you hope and a future." I absolutely held on to that verse.

Talking to Ms. Arwilda was so different than speaking

to an ungodly person, who would just say I needed to leave him or shouldn't let him talk to me like that; it was not that simple. Ms. Arwilda was the one who understood that, and she would continue to encourage me, give me godly advice, and pray for me. Then she talked about a pastor named Dr. David Jeremiah and how she would listen to his sermons.

One day, I decided to look him up. I ended up downloading the Turning Point app on my phone and began to listen to him every night when I took a bath or shower. I honestly enjoyed listening to his sermon every night because it was refreshing and uplifting. It was needed on a daily basis. My husband would get annoyed with me listening to it, but my bath time was me time. He would try to take it away, but I continued to listen to Dr. David Jeremiah. Remember, evil does not want you to get closer to God. As I continued to grow closer to the Lord, my husband would at times persecute me and say that I was hiding behind the Bible. Dr. David Jeremiah (2020) described persecution as a compliment and proof of the faith of the person being persecuted. The enemy felt threatened by my closeness to God. He didn't like it. That just made me more determined to grow closer to the Lord. It is important to know the Word of God and memorize scripture if we are to be victorious against Satan's temptations

There was one time I was in the bathtub and Dr. David Jeremiah was talking about the story of David. He was talking about how King David and his followers had met with Nabal to request some food, and Nabal denied David and his men food. Nabal's wife Abigail heard about what Nabal did and gathered food for David and his men to prevent them from killing her husband. She did not tell her husband what she did. Later Nabal was holding a feast and was drunk, and God struck Nabal dead. When I heard the story, I began crying, asking the Lord to make me like Abigail. I don't wish anyone dead, but I was thinking that would bring me so much relief in my life. I was tired of walking on eggshells every day. I cried out for the Lord to help me.

As much as we may want things to happen immediately, remember, the Lord is not on our timing. When we need God to deliver us from a situation that we know we can't deliver ourselves from, it's clear there is only one thing we can do. No matter how long we have been waiting for a breakthrough, we must be encouraged to keep going, keep asking, and keep knocking, because God is listening (Walsh, 2021).

Eventually, my mornings changed. When I would get up in the morning, I would get dressed and then devote some time to reading the Bible and some devotionals. This truly helped uplift me, especially after a rough night. It is like Lamentations 3:22–23 says: "It is of the Lord's mercies that we are not consumed, because his compassions fail not. They are new every morning: great is thy faithfulness." "New every morning" meant that I shouldn't hold on to anything that happened the night before, but allow myself to wake up refreshed and start a new day with the Lord. Being in an abusive relationship, I had to learn to do this quickly because otherwise I was going to be miserable and depressed. I had children to think about, not just myself, so I learned to wake up each morning starting fresh. My husband found that hard because he would carry something for days.

Little did I know that as I continued to surround myself with the Lord, the Lord was putting me under construction. The Lord was changing my interior design. I began to desire and crave being around godly people like my coworkers, who I could talk to and who had the same perspective as me. I enjoyed being around people who were uplifting, and always gave encouraging words. The Lord began to put more godly people in my life, which was exactly what I needed. I had to deal with so much negativity when I was home, and the positivity was needed to help carry me through to the next day.

Embrace every opportunity you have by listening to sermons or reading a book on prayer or something faith-oriented. I would also use any free time to pray for family and friends, work, and coworkers. I would pray for my husband and my home environment and, of course, my children. Even through my suffering, I wanted to serve God's people more by starting a prayer group, and by sending out daily devotions to fellow believers, family, and friends who I knew needed to hear some encouraging words.

What happens in abusive relationships varies. In some abusive relationships, the man can be very controlling and may not want the woman to work outside of the home. In these cases, it is still possible to surround yourself with God through prayer and reading faith-filled books, and if you have a godly friend or friends to talk to. If possible, get involved in some Bible studies which will allow you to be around other godly people and talk about the Word of God.

As I continued to grow in the Lord, I began to feel more and more that the Lord was going to use me in a way that would include my experiences. Second Corinthians

1:4 states, "who comforts us in all our tribulation, that we may be able to comfort those who are in trouble, with the comfort with which we ourselves are comforted by God." Was that my purpose? Maybe, but there was one thing I had to remember when my eyes were open to recognizing my calling: God was not the only one who knew this. The devil did too, and he was going to do what he could to prevent me from reaching that goal through temptations of my weaknesses. I remember reading a devotional from Dr. Charles Stanley that made me realize and believe in this even more. Do you ever think about how the Lord can bring something good out of illness, unemployment, a broken family, or other difficulties? While we can't always understand what God is doing, there is one thing we can do: trust Him to use our situation for His own glorious purposes. When we view life from God's perspective, every hardship becomes an opportunity to trust His good purpose, fully depend on Him, and respond in a manner that glorifies and exalts Christ (Stanley, 2020, p.33).

In Ecclesiastes 4:10, we read, "For if they fall, the one will lift up his fellow: but woe to him that is alone when he falleth; for he hath not another to help him up." I'm sure most of us have related this verse to having a partner in life, but it is also meant for the people we surround ourselves with. The Lord never intended for us to go through our trials and tribulations alone. The Lord attempts to place other believers in our lives to help support, encourage, and lead us in the direction of the mighty Lord. Don't try to walk this path alone. The Lord intentionally places people in our lives for the extra support and help we need. All you need to do is grab their hands—they are there. I am so thankful for the people the Lord placed in my life to help me through the rough times, which gradually increased as my children got older.

One day, I was reading my morning devotions and I came across a devotion that described pain as a microphone. It described how we should not look at suffering as an obstacle, but as an opportunity to be used by God (Lusko, 2015). As a Christian, there is a guarantee that there will be pain and suffering. We all have a purpose or a mission to fulfill and in order to accomplish that, we must be crushed and pressed if we are to see it. How can we be used in a great way without experiencing the pain (Lusko, 2015)? This makes perfect sense. For me, I know it is much easier to speak to someone who has experienced something similar, because he or she understands what I'm dealing with.

You may be in a bad relationship, but you do not have to face it alone. The Lord has given you help. You're not by yourself—you just have to reach out. There is someone who will grab your hand to help you up when you fall and to encourage you and uplift you. Why would you want to go through this by yourself? The Lord has never left your side. The Lord is just listening and waiting for you to call upon Him. Pray. The Lord is never too busy to listen to your cries.

Mold Me

Happiness is not far away

.All I have to do and say

Lord, I want you in my heart

Here is the place He can start

Lord shape me and mold me

To make me who you want me to be

I'll give it all to you

So I can be free

God you are so good

Good to me

.Now help with the patience and obedience

So you can form me into that person to be

Thank you Lord

Chapter Three

Prayers

IIIIIIIIIIIIIIIIIIIII

Do you think prayer is important? Men and women of the Bible were always known for their prayers to God. David, the man after God's own heart, would pray and talk to the Lord. Daniel prayed three times a day, even when it was forbidden. Throughout Jesus's time on earth, He prayed. We are not above the Lord. Prayer is our intimate communication time to talk, ask, seek, and present our needs, wants, and desires to Him. The Lord enjoys this personal time with us.

Prayer is a very important tool and the key to getting through any situation. Throughout the scriptures, God is constantly commanding us to pray. First Thessalonians 5:17 tells us to "pray without ceasing." "Do not be anxious about anything, but in every situation, by prayer and petition, with thanksgiving, present your requests to God" (Philippians 4:6 NIV). Prayer is our intimate time between us and God. He wants us to lay our concerns on His shoulders, not carry them on ours. When it comes to dealing with an abusive relationship, prayer is extremely important, so we can make it through another day.

During each day of this abusive relationship, I would pray that things would be calm throughout the day. If my husband was going through his rampage, I would pray that the Lord would give me the strength to make it through. I would pray that things would not get violent or destructive because I was the one left cleaning up the mess. At some point, the best we can do isn't good enough to solve our problems. Prayer is the difference between the best you can do and the best God can do (Batterson, 2018; Day 8).

Once we realize how powerful prayer is, we must also remember the purpose of prayer: not to change our circumstances necessarily, but to change us in our circumstances so we can endure and glorify God (Batterson, 2018). "This happened so that the works of God might be displayed in him" (John 9:3 NIV). Batterson (2018) stated that, if you pray to God regularly, irregular things will happen on a regular basis (Day 1).

Prayer does not always have to come from you. I would get people at work, my pastor, family, and friends to continue to pray for me daily. I felt that the more people were praying for me, the better and safer I would be. Prayer is a powerful tool that can be utilized by one or many at once or at different times, all to accomplish the same goal, purpose, or task.

How many times do we ask the Lord to get us out of a certain situation we are in? Sometimes it may feel like the Lord does not hear our prayers or that the Lord is ignoring our cries. Remember, the Lord does hear our prayers, but His view and understanding does not always correlate with ours. The Lord tells us multiple times in His Word to be persistent in prayer (Colossians 4:2; Ephesians 6:18). We are to also pray with an expectant heart and childlike faith. As adults, we try too much to rationalize everything because that is what we do, especially when we become parents. With God, we are not the parents; we are His children. Stop second guessing yourself and come to the Lord with open arms and an open heart.

During these years in this relationship, I became very persistent with my prayers. I was like the parable in the Bible about the widow who continued to seek justice until eventually the judge gave in (Luke 18:1–8). Even in verse 7, the judge says,

> And will not the God bring about justice for His chosen ones, who cry out to Him day and night? Will he keep putting them off? I tell you, He will see that they get justice, and quickly. (NIV)

In 2 Corinthians 12:1–10, Paul spoke about a thorn in the flesh that he asked the Lord to remove, but the Lord refused to remove it and said, "'My grace is sufficient.'" A thorn in the flesh is a point of struggle or suffering we would rather avoid, but God allows it to go on. He uses it to produce in us a humility that leads us to rely on His grace. The Lord is using an abusive relationship to bring you to a point where you are dependent on His grace to see you through each day.

Why do we allow our spouses or significant others to have such a stronghold over us? Second Corinthians 10:3–4 states,

> For though we live in the world, we do not wage war as the world does. The weapons we fight with are not the weapons of the world. On the contrary they have divine power to demolish strongholds.

When we begin praying, we need to pray that these strongholds are broken so they do not have any power over us (Walsh, 2021). Sheila Walsh encourages us to not give up when it comes to praying for a breakthrough. God is listening and it will occur in God's timing (Walsh, 2021).

I started reading books that helped uplift me and encouraged my faith, such as *Divine Revelation of Prayer* by Mary K. Baxter. Dr. David Jeremiah would send out other resources each month. Each of these helped me to evaluate where I was in my walk with the Lord. It helped to give me a sense of hope. I wanted to learn everything about prayer and what I needed to do so my prayers would be answered. One thing I have learned through reading these books is that nothing is too little or too big for our Lord Jesus Christ. The Lord is interested in the smallest thing we could pray about and something that seems outrageous to pray about or for. According to Batterson (2017) in his book *The Circle Maker*, the bolder the prayers, the more they honor God. Batterson (2018) states how "the impossible prayers honor God because they reveal our faith and allow God to reveal His glory" (Day 6).

Prayer was my one way to express my feelings to the Lord and my unhappiness in this marriage. The Lord promised to never give us more than we can bear and that there would be a way to escape (1 Corinthians 10:13). Throughout our marriage, I did pray a lot. Praying was my way of giving my worries and concerns to the Lord and escaping briefly from the reality of what was taking place. After I finally found my way out of the marriage, my prayer life increased.

When we are praying for any given situation, we need to make sure that we truly give it to the Lord, because as humans we tend to pray about it but still hold on to it. At times, we even try to answer our own prayers, but this can delay the Lord's plan (Batterson, 2018). The last thing we want is to delay the escape from an abusive relationship.

Pray

As I walk this weary path
The Lord is never far behind
He is always on my mind
I ask myself which way should I go?
I'm always in between to and fro
Another day has come and gone
Now the sun is rising in the early dawn
Help, help which way do I turn?
To hear your voice is what I yearn
I want to do right by you Lord
To listen and obey
This is why it's so important to always pray

Thank you Lord

Chapter Four

Your Escape

||||||||||||||||||||||||||

Everyone's escape is not going to be the same. Is it a matter of escape mentally, emotionally, and/or physically? The Bible gives instructions on how to escape situations of spiritual danger. God provides a way of escape if we will see it and take it. "Taking it" calls for a choice on our part, a decision of obedience. When the escape door is open, we tend to talk ourselves out of it and form doubt. Then we tend not to take the escape when it is available. We also lose faith and trust in the Lord that He will make a way. Basically, we get scared because we are out of our comfort zones, and we don't know what is going to happen. This is where we need to trust in the Lord with all our hearts and seek His will; the Lord will show us the path to take (Proverbs 3:5–6). We need to trust in the Lord that He will show us where to go and what to do next.

How easy it is to talk ourselves out of our escape. We begin to ask ourselves questions. *Is this what the Lord wants me to do? Will I be able to make it on my own? What am I going to do now? Why do we do this to ourselves?* We begin doubting that we are prepared mentally, emotionally, and physically, and we may even talk ourselves out of using the escape. No matter what, the Lord does not want us to be in a toxic relationship. The Bible does not speak explicitly about domestic violence, but the Word does speak about toxic people and violence and how they create negativity in the environment not only for the individual, but also for children, family, and friends.

In Proverbs 22:24–25 (ESV), we read "Make no friendship with an angry man; and with a furious man thou shalt not go: Lest thou learn his ways and get a snare to thou soul." Proverbs 4:14–17 states, "Enter not into the path of the wicked, and go not in the way of evil men. Avoid it, pass not by it, turn from it, and pass away. For they sleep not, except they have done mischief; and their sleep is taken away, unless they cause some to fall. For they eat the bread of wickedness and drink the wine of violence." The Lord is telling us not to be around evil and to avoid it. If we are married to the evil or living with it, how is that what the Lord wants for us?

There comes a time when we have to make an important decision. We must ask ourselves, *Am I going to take this opportunity to escape, and walk away from this toxic relationship or am I going to stay and be miserable and unhappy for the rest of my life?* Even in the Bible, Jesus demonstrated how to walk away from evil and toxicity. Jesus did not chase after people who would not listen to Him. Why do we choose to chase after men who do not show us respect or give us the love that we need, want, and desire? The big question is this: are we scared of being alone? Would we rather be walking on eggshells every day, or be alone and have peace? "It is better to dwell in a corner of the housetop, than with a brawling woman in a wide house" Proverbs 21:9. It is the same if it's the man who is the nag. I would rather be at peace and alone than live in a house with an abusive husband.

Are we scared of feeling lonely? Loneliness can occur even when we are married. In abusive relationships, this is not an uncommon feeling. I was so lonely in my marriage. Communication was nonexistent. Occasionally, he would talk to me about things that happened to him, but rarely to ask how my day was. That is why I probably enjoyed being at work and being around other godly people. Especially towards the end of my marriage, there were times that I enjoyed being alone. I loved it when my husband wasn't home so I could indulge in some peace of mind—or at least try, because most of the time, the phone calls started.

In 2 Timothy 2:16–17, we read, "But shun profane and vain babblings: for they will increase unto more ungodliness." The Lord did not intend for us to be around evil. Think about where Adam and Eve were living before they sinned: the Garden of Eden. Eden was a beautiful and peaceful garden. The animals and the humans lived as one together. This is what the Lord wanted and intended for us, but we chose something different.

Romans 16:17–18 speaks of division. This is something that occurs often in abusive relationships. My husband brought about much division between me and my family. He basically tried to keep me secluded from family and friends. Honestly, I did not want to be around people and have them hear how he would talk to me, especially if he was in one of his moods; it was quite embarrassing. The last thing I needed was people judging me and looking down upon me. He even tried to divide me and my children, and began pulling me away from them, not wanting me to go to their sporting events and any parent/child events. Thankfully, my eyes were opened, and I decided that I was not going to allow that to take place. My children are my blessings from the Lord (Psalm 127:3), and I was not going to allow him to take that away from me. My children are my world, and I was blessed to be given six of them.

The day I finally escaped from my marriage was when my husband went on a rampage, shoved my daughter up against the wall, tried to get physical with me, and became destructive. I had had enough. He was threatening to destroy my daughter's room on Monday after I left for work. I left in the mornings before my kids left for school, so that was rolling around in my head because I did not know what he would do if I was not there. I called the police. When I called, he left the house, and the police acted like it was a civil matter, and said I had to file for a protective order. That is what I did. I finally took that step, and I must say it was such a relief. I was so proud of myself for finally stepping up for myself and my children. My way of escape finally arrived, and I was going to use it. I listened to Dr. David Jeremiah about using a prayer journal, and I decided to begin my own prayer journal. Our marriage was stressful and overwhelming, but the separation and divorce proceeding were stressful also.

People in abusive relationships are not going to leave until they are ready. Their hearts and minds must be ready to take this step, because it is a big step. The separation and divorce can be just as stressful because the abuser will feel as though he is losing control, which may amp up the hostility and violence. According to Thomas (2019), toxic people are not capable of letting go because they can't stand the thought of someone escaping their wrath. During this time, you will need to constantly be aware of your surroundings. If possible, get a protective order so you can have as much protection for you and the family as possible. I had everyone praying for me and my children during this time, praying for us to be safe, and be watched over and protected.

Throughout this entire time of my escape, the Lord still continued to allow me to be surrounded by godly people. During this time, there was one person who continued to help me and encourage me: Ms. Cindy. Again, she would give me scriptures to help uplift me and I would do the same for her. I looked forward to just talking to her on a regular basis because I knew she understood what I was going through and where I needed to be. Again, through each section of my trials, the Lord continued to provide the support I needed and the encouragement to keep moving forward. When we look back, we can see how the Lord was with us each step of the way.

I was living on the edge because I did not know what he might do. I had to change my locks and keep track of everything, which is what I did. I would keep track of any and all of the texts he would send me. I had to be consistent and persistent. When he would violate the protective order, I filed charges. I was going to make sure he knew that I was not playing his games anymore. He was no longer in control of me. It was time for me to begin playing offense and not defense anymore (Todd, 2021). I was going after the enemy in the name of Jesus. I was not running from him anymore. Going through this trial increased my boldness for Christ, which has continued to increase as He delivered me through it.

If you are going to take this step, you must choose courage over worry. Courage is not the absence of fear; it is the ability to do something that frightens you (Chavez, 2021). You are choosing to place more faith in God than in your Giant (the abuser you are currently with) (Chavez, 2021). Courage is what is needed to take that leap of faith to leave the relationship, if that is what you choose to do. There comes a moment when you must quit talking to God about the mountain in your life and start talking to the mountain about your God (Batterson, 2018).

A Plan

The Lord knew us before we were born
He already had a plan formed
He knew we would make mistakes
And hopefully learn from each one
We end up being harder on ourselves
Than our Lord would ever be
That is why He paid the price at Calvary
The Lord gave each one of us special gifts
He wants us to use them all
Do you realize how much talent there could be?
Amongst a group of believers, including you and me
The Holy Ghost could move and cause disruption
To the devil and all his corruption
I hope you realize how much power each one of us holds
To help the Lord win all of these souls
The Lord planned for us to take different paths
So we may be a witness to people we may pass

Thank you Lord

Chapter Five

Follow Through

||||||||||||||||||||||||

I am sure there will be many things crossing your mind. What do I do now? What will I do without him? Where do I go from here? What is the next step in my journey? You are still wondering if it is real or if it is a dream. I must say the first thing I did was take a big sigh. I needed to see what was going to come next, but I did know one thing for sure: there was no going back!

No matter how long you have been in the abusive relationship, that first step of being on your own will be a big one. For me, I finally felt free to worship and serve the Lord like I had wanted to for so long. I was even more encouraged to do the Lord's work. According to Batterson (2018), we may never feel perfectly ready to move forward with our lives, but this is where we get stuck and don't take any steps forward. There were things I had been wanting to do but could not do because my husband did not like me to be around people or have people at the house, including family members.

Now that I was free, I decided to begin a Bible study, which was something I wanted to do for a while. We were able to have a few sessions before COVID hit. I also started working on my book. The Lord gave me the title of the book and the chapters about a year prior to the separation. I knew I would have to go through some more stages before I would even be able to begin on the book.

No matter what you decide to do—whether you leave or stay in the relationship—please know that your pain has a purpose, and it is not unknown to God (Dooley, 2020). I just hope that you get out of it what the Lord intended and use it, whether to help bring others to Christ or help others through their suffering or other desired outcomes.

In building your faith, 2 Peter 1:5–7 (NIV) advises, "make every effort to add to your faith goodness; and to goodness, knowledge, and to knowledge self-control; and to self-control, perseverance; and to perseverance, godliness; and to godliness, mutual affection, love." Faith is not a one-time event. Growing your faith takes time. It is a process. Think of a baby learning to walk. Is that baby able to walk the first time he or she tries? No. So don't be discouraged. I'm not saying it will not take a lot of trials to grow your faith, but eventually it happens, and you build your trust and believe in God.

Just note that this is only the beginning of the journey. You surrendered your marriage or relationship to the Lord. Now it is time to surrender the rest including your finances, your heart, and yourself. I don't know the path He has for you, but the Lord will prepare you for your journey. As much as the Lord wants to prepare you, you need to be committed to the journey. Each little trial you endure and every encounter you have is a steppingstone to the final destination. According to Dooley (2020), trials force us to move beyond being a surface Christian and force us to live a more committed life with the Lord.

One of my favorite stories is about Joseph. He lived the good life: being favored by his father, having his fancy coat of many colors, and having dreams of his brothers bowing down to him. He was privileged and cocky! This made his siblings so furious with him, they wanted to kill him. They might have if it wasn't for the love for their father, to a certain degree. One day, Joseph's father sent him out to check on his brothers, and guess what? He never came back! Consider Joseph's journey that led him to being second in command to Pharaoh, even while the Lord walked with him. He was sold into slavery, but he did not end up a slave. He was sold to Potiphar, the captain of Pharaoh's guards. Then Joseph was falsely accused by Potiphar's wife and thrown into prison. At times, I know we think what lesson is being in jail teaching. It was a humbling place for Joseph, going from a high to a low.

The Lord continued to prepare Joseph to use the gifts, such as visions and dreams, He had given him. While in jail, Joseph interpreted the baker's and the butler's dreams. Both interpretations came true. Joseph asked the butler not to forget him when he returned to Pharaoh's home. But guess what? Joseph remained in jail for two years. It wasn't until Pharaoh had some dreams that the butler remembered Joseph. Joseph was called from jail to interpret the dreams. When Joseph interpreted Pharaoh's dreams and learned of the famine to come, Pharaoh decided to put someone in charge to help keep things in order. Pharaoh thought there was no better person to coordinate a great plan and keep things in order throughout this famine than the one who interpreted the dream: Joseph. Look back through Joseph's journey. It wasn't just one trial; it was several. It wasn't just a short period of time; it was years. Our years are only days in the Lord's eyes. Our timing is not the Lord's timing. This is a difficult concept for us to grasp at times. But each of these trials served a purpose to get Joseph ready to run and control a kingdom.

I thought that once I made it through the separation and divorce, it would be smooth sailing—not! I was doing well with my family and work, but then the Lord threw in a twist. The Lord decided to let me go through another trial with my finances. Whether as a single parent, and at times even as a married person, my finances have always been tight. After the divorce, however, things finally started to look brighter. The next thing I knew, I found myself underwater with my finances. When I thought it was bad, it got even worse, and that got me thinking.

Instead of praying to Lord to help me, I began asking the Lord, "What do you want me to get out of this or take away from this trial?" Then, one night, I surrendered the last thing I was holding on to, and when I got out of bed, it hit me: *faith*, the substance of things hoped for, the evidence of things not seen. The Lord was teaching me to have complete faith in Him. "Lord, I surrender" was all I could say. Why do we feel like we can release parts of our lives to the Lord, but not the rest? Sometimes there are parts of our lives that we try to hold on to and have a difficult time releasing. By holding on to parts or not releasing them wholeheartedly to God, sometimes we can cause things to be harder than intended.

At times we make things more difficult for ourselves by not surrendering and being obedient to the task the Lord is asking us to do. Look at the story of Jonah. The Lord told Jonah to go to Nineveh to preach the gospel, but what did Jonah do instead? He ran in the opposite direction. We all know what happened to Jonah. He boarded a ship, which went through a terrible storm, and the men on the ship thought they were going to die. Jonah admitted that he was the reason this was taking place, so he told the men to throw him overboard. Then Jonah was swallowed by a large fish, and he stayed inside the fish for three days before being spewed out by the fish on the dry land. Finally, Jonah went to Nineveh. Why do we run from God? Where does it get us? We tend to bring more pain and difficulties on ourselves when we are not obedient and instead run away from God's calling.

Why is letting go so difficult for abused women? For women in abusive relationships, the hardest thing for them to let go of is themselves. The husband or significant other is always trying to control what we do, where we go, how we think, how we react and respond, so the last thing we want to do is let go of ourselves and our hearts. This can be difficult for abused women to do because we are trying to regain our independence, not be controlled again. What we fail to forget is God is not a man, but our Lord and Savior. He is here to give us life and more abundantly, not control us. The Lord has always given us free choice. The great example is Adam and Eve in the garden of Eden. They were told not to eat from the forbidden tree, but they did it anyway. The Lord could have stopped them, but He didn't.

I hope in the end you become bolder in Christ, that you have learned the purpose of this trial, and that you continue to move forward with God wholeheartedly. Don't ever give up in your journey, or think that God has abandoned you, because He hasn't. He is still right there by your side, waiting for you to follow Him with all of yourself. God wants what's best for us and He wants to bless us abundantly. Keep Romans 8:28 in mind through all of this: "And we know that all things work together for good to them that love God, to them who are called according to His purpose."

Simple Things
God is so awesome
So merciful, meek, and humble
He is always there to catch us when we tumble
He will provide for all of our needs
And give us the desires of our heart
Here and now is the place you can start
We make things so complicated
This is why to the Lord we need to be dedicated
We need to enjoy the simple things in life
Family, friends, and everyday strife
We need to take it in stride
And put the anger and bitterness to the side
Look at Adam and Eve in the Garden of Eden
Walking around enjoying their freedom
Until the evil snake came and took it all away.
On the straight and narrow pathway
Is where we need to stay
How does it feel to have everything you want
But not have a place for your soul
You feel miserable and unhappy and never satisfied
You try to push all these feelings to the side
God is encouraging, helpful, and uplifting
God is always very forgiving
We all take wrong turns and fall here and there
But God is there to pick us up
When we call out to Him in time of prayer
Thank You Lord

References

Batterson, Mark. 2018. *Draw the circle prayer journal: A 40 day experiment.* Grand Rapids, MI: Zondervan.

Batterson, Mark. 2017. *The circle maker: praying circles around your biggest dreams and greatest fears.* Grand Rapids, MI: Zondervan.

Chavez, Jabin., 2021. *Ridiculous Reality.* Elevation Church.

Dooley, Adam B. 2020. *Hope When Life Unravels: Finding God When It Hurts.* Grand Rapids, MI: Zondervan.

Furtick, Steven. 2019. *When the battle chooses you.* Elevation Church.

Jeremiah, David. 2020. *How to be happy according to Jesus. The study of the beatitudes.*

Lusko, Levi. 2015. *Through the eyes of a lion: Facing impossible pain, finding incredible power.*

New York, NY: Harper Collins Publishing.

Mohler. Albert. 2019. *Prayer that turns the world upside down: The lord 's prayer as a manifesto for revolution.* Nashville, TN: Thomas Nelson Publishing.

Stanley, Charles. 2020. *Blessed to be.* In Touch Ministries, p.33.

Thomas, Gary. 2019. *When to Walk Away.* Grand Rapids, MI: Zondervan.

Todd, Michael. 2021. *It's time to stop playing defense.* Transformation Church.

Walsh, Sheila. 2021. *Pray through to breakthrough.* https://sheilawalsh.com/pray-through-to-breakthrough/.

Printed in the United States
by Baker & Taylor Publisher Services